CATS LOVE CHRISTMAS TOO

A SEASONAL CELEBRATION
IN POETRY AND PROSE

Illuminated by Isabelle Brent

Little, Brown and Company
BOSTON • NEW YORK • TORONTO • LONDON

For Little Cat, Teasel, Sappho, Lancôme, Seolta, Bat,
Whiskers, Scrappety, Ferdinand, Poppy and Ruddles

A LITTLE, BROWN BOOK

First published in Great Britain in 1996 by Little, Brown and Company (UK)

Conceived, designed and produced by
The Albion Press Limited
Spring Hill, Idbury, Oxfordshire OX7 6RU

Illustrations copyright © 1996 by Isabelle Brent
Selection copyright © 1996 by The Albion Press Ltd
Volume copyright © 1996 by The Albion Press Ltd
Text copyright © 1996 individual sources as noted below. All rights reserved. Used by permission.

We would like to thank all the authors, publishers and literary representatives who have given permission to reproduce work in this collection. Every effort has been made to contact copyright holders. We will be glad to make good any errors or omissions in future editions.

Elizabeth Coatsworth: to Catherine B. Barnes for "On a Night of Snow" from NIGHT AND THE CAT (Macmillan N.Y., 1950).

D. H. Lawrence: to Viking Penguin, a division of Penguin Books USA Inc., for "Pax" from the COMPLETE POEMS OF D. H. LAWRENCE by D. H. Lawrence, edited by V. de Sola Pinto & F. W. Roberts. Copyright © 1964, 1971 by Angelo Ravagli and C. M. Weekley, Executors of the Estate of Frieda Lawrence Ravagli. Used by permission.

Myra Cohn Livingston: to Simon and Schuster Inc. and to Marian Reiner for the author for "Kittens" from WORLDS I KNOW AND OTHER POEMS by Myra Cohn Livingston. Copyright © 1985 Myra Cohn Livingston. A Margaret K. McElderry Book for Atheneum.

Beatrix Potter: to Frederick Warne & Co for an extract from THE TAILOR OF GLOUCESTER by Beatrix Potter. Copyright © F. Warne & Co., 1903.

Stevie Smith: to James MacGibbon, Executor of the Estate of Stevie Smith, for "The Singing Cat" from THE COLLECTED POEMS OF STEVIE SMITH (Penguin 20th Century Classics), and to New Directions Publishing Corporation for "The Singing Cat" from COLLECTED POEMS OF STEVIE SMITH. Copyright © 1972 by Stevie Smith.

ISBN 0-316-91122-4

A CIP catalogue record for this book is available from the British Library

1   3   5   7   9   10   8   6   4   2

Printed and bound in Hong Kong

Little, Brown and Company (UK)
Brettenham House, Lancaster Place
London WC2E 7EN

CONTENTS

ON A NIGHT OF SNOW

Cat, if you go outdoors you must walk in the snow.
You will come back with little white shoes on your feet,
Little white slippers of snow that have heels of sleet.
Stay by the fire, my Cat. Lie still, do not go.
See how the flames are leaping and hissing low,
I will bring you a saucer of milk like a marguerite,
So white and so smooth, so spherical and so sweet —
Stay with me, Cat. Outdoors the wild winds blow.

Outdoors the wild winds blow, Mistress, and dark is the night.
Strange voices cry in the trees, intoning strange lore;
And more than cats move, lit by our eyes' green light,
On silent feet where the meadow grasses hang hoar —
Mistress, there are portents abroad of magic and might,
And things that are yet to be done. Open the door!

Elizabeth Coatsworth

DANIEL

Daniel the cat speaks
hopefully of bringing me a nice fat robin
on Xmas morning, but I
discourage this light way of thinking . . .

M. R. James

CHRISTMAS NIGHT

But it is in the old story that all the beasts can talk, in the night between Christmas Eve and Christmas Day in the morning (though there are very few folk that can hear them, or know what it is that they say).

When the Cathedral clock struck twelve there was an answer — like an echo of the chimes — and Simpkin heard it, and came out of the tailor's door, and wandered about in the snow.

From all the roofs and gables and old wooden houses in Gloucester came a thousand merry voices singing the old Christmas rhymes — all the old songs that ever I heard of, and some that I don't know; like Whittington's bells.

First and loudest the cocks cried out "Dame, get up and bake your pies!"

"Oh, dilly, dilly, dilly!" sighed Simpkin.

And now in a garret there were lights and sounds of dancing, and cats came from over the way.

"Hey, diddle, diddle, the cat and the fiddle! All the cats in Gloucester — except me," said Simpkin.

Under the wooden eaves the starlings and sparrows sang of Christmas pies; the jackdaws woke up in the Cathedral tower; and although it was the middle of the night the throstles and robins sang; the air was quite full of little twittering tunes.

But it was all rather provoking for poor hungry Simpkin.

Beatrix Potter

THE SINGING CAT

It was a little captive cat
   Upon a crowded train
His mistress takes him from his box
   To ease his fretful pain.

She holds him tight upon her knee
   The graceful animal
And all the people look at him
   He is so beautiful.

But oh he pricks and oh he prods
   And turns upon her knee
Then lifteth up his innocent voice
   In plaintive melody.

He lifteth up his innocent voice
   He lifteth up, he singeth
And to each human countenance
   A smile of grace he bringeth.

He lifteth up his innocent paw
   Upon her breast he clingeth
And everybody cries, Behold
   The cat, the cat that singeth.

He lifteth up his innocent voice
   He lifteth up, he singeth
And all the people warm themselves
   In the love his beauty bringeth.

Stevie Smith

PUSSY CAT SITS BY THE FIRE

Pussy cat sits by the fire;
   How did she come there?
In walks the little dog,
   Says, "Pussy! Are you there?"

"How do you do, Mistress Pussy?
   Mistress Pussy, how d'ye do?"
"I thank you kindly, little dog,
   I fare as well as you!"

Traditional

CHRISTMAS IN THE WHITE HOUSE
1902

There was also one present each for Jack the dog, Tom Quarz the kitten, and Algonquin the pony. . . . Tom Quartz is certainly the cunningest kitten I have ever seen. He is always playing pranks on Jack and I get very nervous lest Jack should grow too irritated. The other evening they were both in the library — Jack sleeping before the fire — Tom Quartz scampering about, an exceedingly playful little wild creature — which is about what he is. He would race across the floor, then jump upon the curtain or play with the tassel. Suddenly he spied Jack and galloped up to him. Jack, looking exceedingly sullen and shame-faced, jumped out of the way and got upon the sofa, where Tom Quartz instantly jumped upon him again. Jack suddenly shifted to the other sofa, where Tom Quartz again went after him. Then Jack started for the door, while Tom made a rapid turn under the sofa and around the table, and just as Jack reached the door leaped on his hind-quarters. Jack bounded forward and away and the two went tandem out of the room — Jack not reappearing at all; and after about five minutes Tom Quartz stalked solemnly back.

Theodore Roosevelt

SNOW IN THE SUBURBS

Every branch big with it,
Bent every twig with it;
Every fork like a white web-foot;
Every street and pavement mute:
Some flakes have lost their way, and grope back upward, when
Meeting those meandering down they turn and descend again.
The palings are glued together like a wall,
And there is no waft of wind with the fleecy fall.

A sparrow enters the tree,
Whereon immediately
A snow-lump thrice his own slight size
Descends on him and showers his head and eyes,
And overturns him,
And near inurns him,
And lights on a nether twig, when its brush
Starts off a volley of other lodging lumps with a rush.

The steps are a blanched slope
Up which, with feeble hope,
A black cat comes, wide-eyed and thin;
And we take him in.

Thomas Hardy

KITTENS

Our cat had kittens
weeks ago
when everything outside was snow.

So she stayed in
and kept them warm
and safe from all the clouds and storm.

But yesterday
when there was sun
she snuzzled on the smallest one

and turned it over
from beneath
and took its fur between her teeth

and carried it
outside to see
how nice a winter day can be

and then our dog
decided he
would help her take the other three

and one by one
they took them out
to see what sun is all about

so when they're grown
they'll always know
to never be afraid of snow.

Myra Cohn Livingston

THE KING OF THE CATS

One Christmas night — and a wild, stormy night it was — a farmer was making his way home across the fields when a cat came up to him, bold as brass, and called out, "Tell Dildrum, Doldrum's dead!"

Well, he went on his way. When he got home, he joined his wife where she sat by the fire, with their big old black cat by her side.

"You'll never guess what happened to me this night," he said. "A cat spoke to me!"

His wife looked up at that, and so did the cat. "Spoke to you?" she said.

"As plain as you. It said, 'Tell Dildrum, Doldrum's dead!'"

The old black cat arched his back, and sparks seemed to flash from his eyes. "What!" he cried. "Is old Doldrum dead? Then I'm the King of the Cats!" And with that he shot up the chimney, and they never saw him again.

Traditional

From JUBILATE AGNO

For I will consider my Cat Jeoffrey.
For he is the servant of the Living God,
    duly and daily serving him.
For at the First glance of the glory of God in the East
    he worships in his way.
For is this done by wreathing his body seven times round
    with elegant quickness.
For then he leaps up to catch the musk,
    which is the blessing of God upon his prayer.
For he is of the tribe of Tiger.
For the Cherub Cat is a term of the Angel Tiger.
For he has the subtlety and hissing of a serpent,
    which in goodness he suppresses.
For he will not do destruction, if he is well fed,
    neither will he spit without provocation.
For he purrs in thankfulness,
    when God tells him he's a good Cat.
For he is an instrument for the children
    to learn benevolence upon.
For every house is incomplete without him
    and a blessing is lacking in the spirit.

Christopher Smart

PAX

All that matters is to be at one with the living God
to be a creature in the house of the God of Life.

Like a cat asleep on a chair
at peace, in peace
and at one with the master of the house, with the mistress,
at home, at home in the house of the living,
sleeping on the hearth, and yawning before the fire.

Sleeping on the hearth of the living world
yawning at home before the fire of life
feeling the presence of the living God
like a great reassurance
a deep calm in the heart
a presence
as of the master sitting at the board
in his own and greater being,
in the house of life.

D. H. Lawrence